GOSPEL GREATS

15 SONGS OF FAITH ARRANGED BY PHILLIP

T0071503

CONTENTS

— PIANO LEVEL —
LATE INTERMEDIATE/EARLY ADVANCED

ISBN 978-1-4950-1724-7

HAL•LEONARD®
CORPORATION

7777 W. BLUEMOUND RD. P.O. BOX 13819 MILWAUKEE, WI 53213

Visit Hal Leonard Online at
www.halleonard.com

Visit Phillip at
www.phillipkeveren.com

PREFACE

This is a power-punching collection of songs! There are no fillers here, to be sure. Every one of these songs has been a vital part of gospel music for many years. Their melodies and lyrics have rung out in cavernous stadiums to small, intimate churches the world over – touching the hearts and souls of millions of listeners.

I have played most of these songs as piano solos at some time or another over the decades. The arrangements within were all penned afresh, but they carry harmonies and interpretive elements that have evolved in my fingers over many years.

It is a privilege to have the opportunity to arrange these gospel greats for you.

Sincerely,

Phillip Keveren

◆

BIOGRAPHY

Phillip Keveren, a multi-talented keyboard artist and composer, has composed original works in a variety of genres from piano solo to symphonic orchestra. Mr. Keveren gives frequent concerts and workshops for teachers and their students in the United States, Canada, Europe, and Asia. Mr. Keveren holds a B.M. in composition from California State University Northridge and a M.M. in composition from the University of Southern California.

THE FAMILY OF GOD

Words and Music by WILLIAM J. GAITHER
and GLORIA GAITHER
Arranged by Phillip Keveren

BECAUSE HE LIVES

Words and Music by WILLIAM J. GAITHER
and GLORIA GAITHER
Arranged by Phillip Keveren

Expressively, with freedom (♩ = 100)

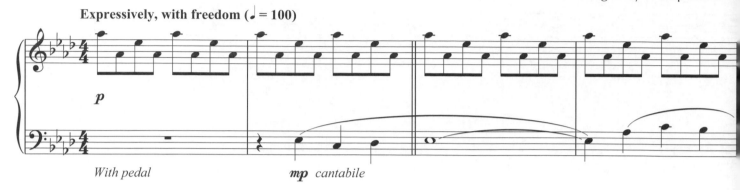

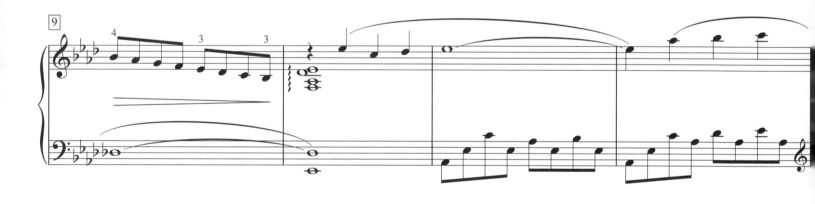

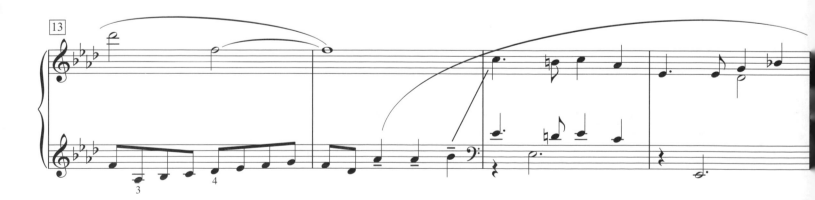

With strength (♩ = 96)

HE TOUCHED ME

Words and Music by
WILLIAM J. GAITHER
Arranged by Phillip Keveren

Freely expressive (♩ = 96)

With pedal

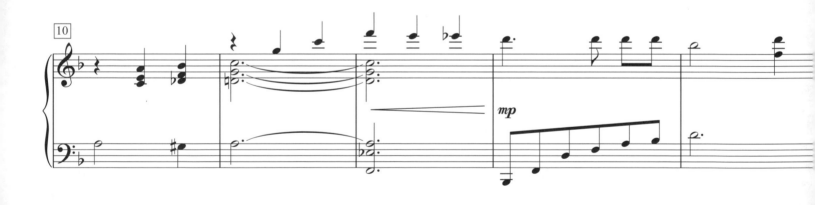

HIS EYE IS ON THE SPARROW

Words by CIVILLA D. MARTIN
Music by CHARLES H. GABRIEL
Arranged by Phillip Keveren

HOW GREAT THOU ART

Words by STUART K. HINE
Swedish Folk Melody Adapted and Arranged by
STUART K. HINE
Arranged by Phillip Keverer

I'D RATHER HAVE JESUS

Words by RHEA F. MILLER
Music by GEORGE BEVERLY SHEA
Arranged by Phillip Keveren

Gently (♩ = 92-96)

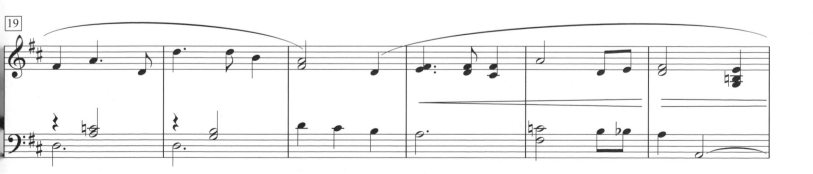

I SAW THE LIGHT

Words and Music by
HANK WILLIAMS
Arranged by Phillip Keveren

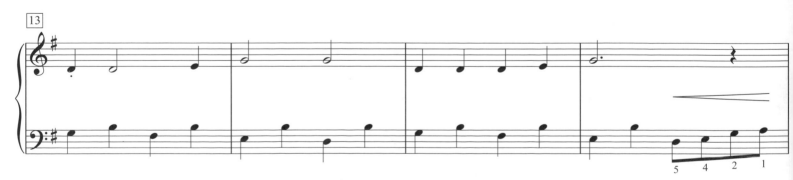

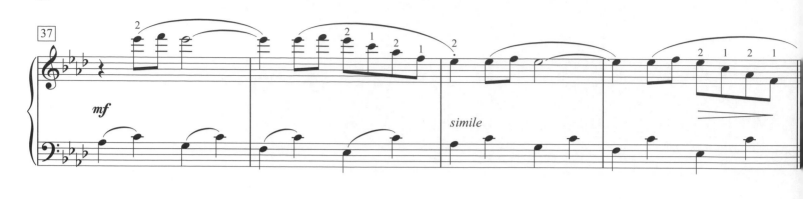

I'LL FLY AWAY

Words and Music by
ALBERT E. BRUMLEY
Arranged by Phillip Keveren

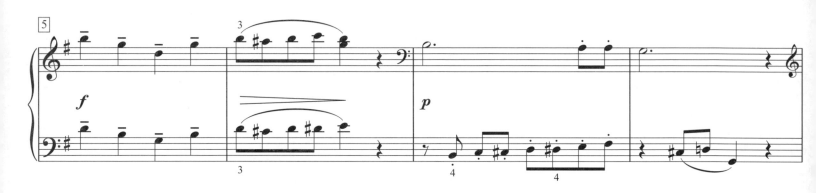

MORE THAN WONDERFUL

Words and Music by
LANNY WOLFE
Arranged by Phillip Keveren

MY TRIBUTE

Words and Music by
ANDRAÉ CROUCH
Arranged by Phillip Keveren

PRECIOUS LORD, TAKE MY HAND

(Take My Hand, Precious Lord)

Words and Music by
THOMAS A. DORSEY
Arranged by Phillip Keveren

With pedal

VICTORY IN JESUS

Words and Music by
E.M. BARTLETT
Arranged by Phillip Keveren

WE SHALL BEHOLD HIM

Words and Music by
DOTTIE RAMBO
Arranged by Phillip Keveren

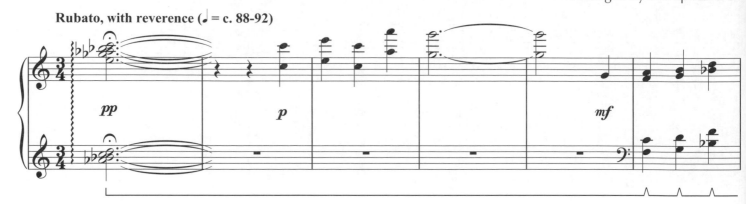

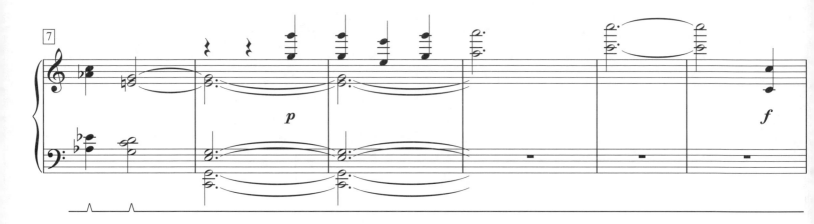

WILL THE CIRCLE BE UNBROKEN

Words by ADA R. HABERSHON
Music by CHARLES H. GABRIEL
Arranged by Phillip Keveren

SOON AND VERY SOON

Words and Music by
ANDRAÉ CROUCH
Arranged by Phillip Keveren